Francis Frith's
COUNTY DURHAM

PHOTOGRAPHIC MEMORIES

Francis Frith's
COUNTY DURHAM

◆

Clive Hardy

FRITH
BOOK Co

First published in the United Kingdom in 2000 by
Frith Book Company Ltd

Hardback Edition 2000
ISBN 1-85937-123-x

Paperback Edition 2001
ISBN 1-85937-398-4

Reprinted in Hardback 2001
ISBN 1-85937-123-x

British Library Cataloguing in Publication Data

County Durham
Clive Hardy

Frith Book Company Ltd
Frith's Barn, Teffont,
Salisbury, Wiltshire SP3 5QP
Tel: +44 (0) 1722 716 376
Email: info@francisfrith.co.uk
www.francisfrith.co.uk

Printed and bound in Great Britain

Contents

Francis Frith: *Victorian Pioneer*

FRANCIS FRITH, Victorian founder of the world-famous photographic archive, was a complex and multitudinous man. A devout Quaker and a highly successful Victorian businessman, he was both philosophic by nature and pioneering in outlook.

By 1855 Francis Frith had already established a wholesale grocery business in Liverpool, and sold it for the astonishing sum of £200,000, which is the equivalent today of over £15,000,000. Now a multi-millionaire, he was able to indulge his passion for travel. As a child he had pored over travel books written by early explorers, and his fancy and imagination had been stirred by family holidays to the sublime mountain regions of Wales and Scotland. 'What a land of spirit-stirring and enriching scenes and places!' he had written. He was to return to these scenes of grandeur in later years to 'recapture the thousands of vivid and tender memories', but with a different purpose. Now in his thirties, and captivated by the new science of photography, Frith set out on a series of pioneering journeys to the Nile regions that occupied him from 1856 until 1860.

Intrigue and Adventure

He took with him on his travels a specially-designed wicker carriage that acted as both dark-room and sleeping chamber. These far-flung journeys were packed with intrigue and adventure. In his life story, written when he was sixty-three, Frith tells of being held captive by bandits, and of fighting 'an awful midnight battle to the very point of surrender with a deadly pack of hungry, wild dogs'. Sporting flowing Arab costume, Frith arrived at Akaba by camel seventy years before Lawrence, where he encountered 'desert princes and rival sheikhs, blazing with jewel-hilted swords'.

During these extraordinary adventures he was assiduously exploring the desert regions bordering the Nile and patiently recording the antiquities and peoples with his camera. He was the first photographer to venture beyond the sixth cataract. Africa was still the mysterious 'Dark Continent', and Stanley and Livingstone's historic meeting was a decade into the future. The conditions for picture taking confound belief. He laboured for hours in his wicker dark-room in the sweltering heat of the desert, while the volatile chemicals fizzed dangerously in their trays. Often he was forced to work in remote tombs and caves where conditions were cooler. Back in London he exhibited his photographs and was 'rapturously cheered' by members of the Royal Society. His reputation as a photographer was made overnight. An eminent modern historian has likened their impact on the population of the time to that on our own generation of the first photographs taken on the surface of the moon.

Venture of a Life-Time

Characteristically, Frith quickly spotted the opportunity to create a new business as a specialist publisher of photographs. He lived in an era of immense and sometimes violent change. For the poor in the early part of Victoria's reign work was a drudge and the hours long, and people had precious little free time to enjoy themselves. Most had no transport other than a cart or gig at their disposal, and had not travelled far beyond the boundaries of their own town or village.

However, by the 1870s, the railways had threaded their way across the country, and Bank Holidays and half-day Saturdays had been made obligatory by Act of Parliament. All of a sudden the ordinary working man and his family were able to enjoy days out and see a little more of the world.

With characteristic business acumen, Francis Frith foresaw that these new tourists would enjoy having souvenirs to commemorate their days out. In 1860 he married Mary Ann Rosling and set out with the intention of photographing every city, town and village in Britain. For the next thirty years he travelled the country by train and by pony and trap, producing fine photographs of seaside resorts and beauty spots that were keenly bought by millions of Victorians. These prints were painstakingly pasted into family albums and pored over during the dark nights of winter, rekindling precious memories of summer excursions.

The Rise of Frith & Co

Frith's studio was soon supplying retail shops all over the country. To meet the demand he gathered about him a small team of photographers, and published the work of independent artist-photographers of the calibre of Roger Fenton and Francis Bedford. In order to gain some understanding of the scale of Frith's business one only has to look at the catalogue issued by Frith & Co in 1886: it runs to some 670 pages, listing not only many thousands of views of the British Isles but also many photographs of most European countries, and China, Japan, the USA and Canada – note the sample page shown above

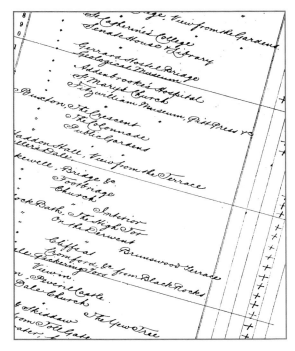

from the hand-written *Frith & Co* ledgers detailing pictures taken. By 1890 Frith had created the greatest specialist photographic publishing company in the world, with over 2,000 outlets – more than the combined number that Boots and WH Smith have today! The picture on the right shows the *Frith & Co* display board at Ingleton in the Yorkshire Dales. Beautifully constructed with mahogany frame and gilt inserts, it could display up to a dozen local scenes.

Postcard Bonanza

The ever-popular holiday postcard we know today took many years to develop. In 1870 the Post Office issued the first plain cards, with a pre-printed stamp on one face. In 1894 they allowed other publishers' cards to be sent through the mail with an attached adhesive halfpenny stamp. Demand grew rapidly, and in 1895 a new size of postcard was permitted

called the court card, but there was little room for illustration. In 1899, a year after Frith's death, a new card measuring 5.5 x 3.5 inches became the standard format, but it was not until 1902 that the divided back came into being, with address and message on one face and a full-size illustration on the other. *Frith & Co* were in the vanguard of postcard development, and Frith's sons Eustace and Cyril continued their father's monumental task, expanding the number of views offered to the public and recording more and more places in Britain, as the coasts and countryside were opened up to mass travel.

Francis Frith died in 1898 at his villa in Cannes, his great project still growing. The archive he created continued in business for another seventy years. By 1970 it contained over a third of a million pictures of 7,000 cities, towns and villages. The massive photographic record Frith has left to us stands as a living monument to a special and very remarkable man.

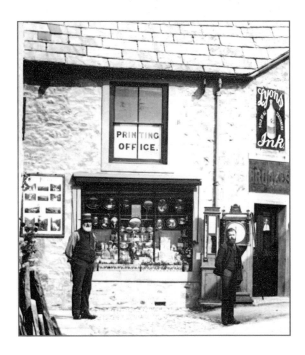

Frith's Archive: *A Unique Legacy*

FRANCIS FRITH'S legacy to us today is of immense significance and value, for the magnificent archive of evocative photographs he created provides a unique record of change in 7,000 cities, towns and villages throughout Britain over a century and more. Frith and his fellow studio photographers revisited locations many times down the years to update their views, compiling for us an enthralling and colourful pageant of British life and character.

We tend to think of Frith's sepia views of Britain as nostalgic, for most of us use them to conjure up memories of places in our own lives with which we have family associations. It often makes us forget that to Francis Frith they were records of daily life as it was actually being lived in the cities, towns and villages of his day. The Victorian age was one of great and often bewildering change for ordinary people, and

See Frith at www.francisfrith.co.uk

though the pictures evoke an impression of slower times, life was as busy and hectic as it is today.

We are fortunate that Frith was a photographer of the people, dedicated to recording the minutiae of everyday life. For it is this sheer wealth of visual data, the painstaking chronicle of changes in dress, transport, street layouts, buildings, housing, engineering and landscape that captivates us so much today. His remarkable images offer us a powerful link with the past and with the lives of our ancestors.

Today's Technology

Computers have now made it possible for Frith's many thousands of images to be accessed almost instantly. In the Frith archive today, each photograph is carefully 'digitised' then stored on a CD Rom. Frith archivists can locate a single photograph amongst thousands within seconds. Views can be catalogued and sorted under a variety of categories of place and content to the immediate benefit of researchers.

Inexpensive reference prints can be created for them at the touch of a mouse button, and a wide range of books and other printed materials assembled and published for a wider, more general readership - in the next twelve months over a hundred Frith local history titles will be published! The day-to-day workings of the archive are very different from how they were in Francis Frith's time: imagine the herculean task of sorting through eleven tons of glass negatives as Frith had to do to locate a particular sequence of pictures! Yet the archive still prides itself on maintaining the same high standards of excellence laid down by Francis Frith, including the painstaking cataloguing and indexing of every view.

It is curious to reflect on how the internet now allows researchers in America and elsewhere greater instant access to the archive than Frith himself ever enjoyed. Many thousands of individual views can be called up on screen within seconds on one of the Frith internet sites, enabling people living continents away to revisit the streets of their ancestral home town, or view places in Britain where they have enjoyed holidays. Many overseas researchers welcome the chance to view special theme selections, such as transport, sports, costume and ancient monuments.

We are certain that Francis Frith would have heartily approved of these modern developments in imaging techniques, for he himself was always working at the very limits of Victorian photographic technology.

The Value of the Archive Today

Because of the benefits brought by the computer, Frith's images are increasingly studied by social historians, by researchers into genealogy and ancestry, by architects, town planners, and by teachers and schoolchildren involved in local history projects.

In addition, the archive offers every one of us an opportunity to examine the places where we and our families have lived and worked down the years. Highly successful in Frith's own era, the archive is now, a century and more on, entering a new phase of popularity.

The Past in Tune with the Future

Historians consider the Francis Frith Collection to be of prime national importance. It is the only archive of its kind remaining in private ownership and has been valued at a million pounds. However, this figure is now rapidly increasing as digital technology enables more and more people around the world to enjoy its benefits.

Francis Frith's archive is now housed in an historic timber barn in the beautiful village of Teffont in Wiltshire. Its founder would not recognize the archive office as it is today. In place of the many thousands of dusty boxes containing glass plate negatives and an all-pervading odour of photographic chemicals, there are now ranks of computer screens. He would be amazed to watch his images travelling round the world at unimaginable speeds through network and internet lines.

The archive's future is both bright and exciting. Francis Frith, with his unshakeable belief in making photographs available to the greatest number of people, would undoubtedly approve of what is being done today with his lifetime's work. His photographs, depicting our shared past, are now bringing pleasure and enlightenment to millions around the world a century and more after his death.

COUNTY DURHAM - *An Introduction*

COUNTY DURHAM'S BORDERS once extended from the south bank of the Tyne to the north bank of the Tees; the western border extended into the Pennines, the north-western along the banks of the Derwent. It was a county of contrasts, looking surprisingly agricultural to outsiders, who imagined nothing but coal mines, slag heaps, steelworks, quarries, shipyards and heavy industry. There were indeed plenty of collieries as well; swhen the NCB was formed in 1947, there were 127 active pits employing 108,000 mine workers, and there were shipyards along the Durham side of the Tyne, and along the Wear and the Tees. In 1974, however, as a result of changes in local government boundaries, Durham lost considerable chunks of territory and much of its industrial base to the newly-created authorities of Tyne & Wear and Cleveland, though it gained Startforth Rural District from the North Riding of Yorkshire. As a result, Durham lost half of its population, and its coastline was reduced to a mere eleven miles in length.

It goes without saying that this is a part of England steeped in history. Along with Yorkshire, it once formed the powerful Anglo-Saxon kingdom of Northumbria. With its capital at York, by the early 7th century Northumbria extended from the Forth to the Humber and the north bank of the Mersey. Indeed, it is thought that Edinburgh was founded in the 7th century by King Edwin. It is known that Edwin fortified a part of the hill where the present-day Edinburgh Castle stands, and he may also have encouraged civilian settlement nearby. Under another 7th-century

king, Aethelfrith, Northumbria was powerful enough to launch an all-out assault on the city of Chester in 616 and hold onto it for about thirty years.

Northumbria also became one of the great centres of early Christianity following the conversion of King Oswald whilst he was in exile in Scotland; it was he who founded Lindisfarne in 635. Other 7th-century Northumbrian monasteries include Hartlepool (647), Whitby (657), Monkwearmouth (674), and Jarrow (681). Jarrow is for ever associated with Bede, the scholar, historian and grammarian; he wrote 79 books, the most famous of which is his 'Ecclesiastical History of the English People'. Bede wrote in both Latin and Anglo-Saxon, and his scholarship brought him international recognition. Bede died in 735 aged 62, having just completed a translation into Anglo-Saxon of St John's Gospel. He was buried at Jarrow in a special porch on the north side of the monastery church, but his remains were later interred under the high altar. In the 11th century his remains were moved to Durham, where they now rest in a black, marble-topped tomb in the Galilee Chapel.

In 875 the Community of St Cuthbert finally abandoned Lindisfarne to the invading Danes; carrying their saint's bones, they sought safety elsewhere. After several years of wandering around Northumbria, the Community finally settled at Chester-le-Street in 883, and St Cuthbert was laid to rest in the Saxon church there. In 995, with the threat of further Viking raids looming, the Community were once more on the move. It is said that the saint himself intervened in the selection of Durham as a permanent resting place, but the defensive qualities of a peninsula with high steep banks and almost completely surrounded by water would not have been lost on the monks. There was already an Anglo-Saxon settlement on the peninsula when the Community arrived, and a wattle church already existed on the site now occupied by St Mary-le-Bow. The Palatinate may have its origins in grants and privileges that pre-date the Norman Conquest, those made by King Egfrith to Cuthbert himself on his elevation to the see of Lindisfarne in 685. There appear to have been further grants of land by Guthred the Dane and Alfred the Great, and these were ratified by William the Conqueror.

It was under Norman rule that Durham became an important administrative centre; William the Conqueror granted it the status of a palatinate as a buffer against the Scots. It was ruled over by capable warrior-bishops who were free to raise taxes, maintain armies, wage war and enjoy almost complete independence from the English crown. When Bishop Aethelwin, a Saxon, died he was succeeded by a Norman, Walcher of Lorraine. In 1076 Walcher was also created Earl of

Northumberland following the execution of Waltheof for conspiracy against William, and for the first time two of the most important and most powerful titles in the North were held by one man.

The relationship between England, Scotland, and the palatinate were a little fluid - the armies of both crowns appear at times to have enjoyed free passage through the bishop's territory. During the reign of William Rufus, England's northern frontier might well have followed the line of Hadrian's Wall; its focal points were the fortresses of Carlisle in the west, and the New Castle on the north bank of the Tyne over to the east. The castle on the Tyne had been built by Robert Curthose, the brave but short-tempered and headstrong eldest son of the Conqueror, on his return from campaigning against Malcolm III of Scotland.

Hugh le Puiset was created Bishop of Durham in 1153. Such was his independent streak that in 1173 he entered into a secret treaty with William the Lion of Scotland. During the reign of David I, the peace treaty following the Battle of the Standard (in which he had been defeated) still resulted in his son Henry being granted the earldom of Northumbria, but without any claims to the territory of St Cuthbert. Later, when Henry II of England insisted that Northumbria be returned, William the Lion launched an invasion aided by le Puiset. The Scots were granted the fortress of Northallerton, an outpost of the palatinate in Yorkshire, and free passage for their troops. French and Flemish allies of the Scots were allowed to use the port of Hartlepool. However, William the Lion was captured at Alnwick and taken to the fortress of Falaise in Normandy. William bowed to the inevitable; he acknowledged Henry as his feudal lord, and ceded several castles in southern Scotland to the English. Bishop le Puiset was punished by being heavily fined and having the castles of Durham, Northallerton and Norham temporarily confiscated.

On a more benevolent note, Bishop le Puiset was responsible for building Elvet Bridge in Durham, thereby providing the peninsula with direct road access to the south; he also founded Sherburn Hospital in about 1181 for the treatment of lepers. In 1183 le Puiset ordered the equivalent of a Domesday survey of the palatinate. Details relating to the village of Boldon form the first substantial entry, and the survey became known as the Boldon Book.

Another independent bishop was Anthony Bek, who reigned between 1284 and 1310. He was also Lord of Man, Patriarch of Jerusalem, and a talented soldier. He was a contemporary of Edward Longshanks, probably the most ruthless and most able king ever to sit upon the throne of England. In 1296, Bek actively supported

Longshanks when he stripped John Baliol of the Scottish throne for failing to attend the parliament at Newcastle. Two years later, Bek commanded a wing of the English army at Falkirk; yet he opposed the right of visitation claimed by the archbishops of York, and supported the Nevilles when they contested Longshanks's right to call on palatinate troops for service beyond its borders. There were times, however, when the English crown took an active role in the selection of the bishop. In 1328, when the monks of Durham chose Thomas de Melsanby as bishop, Henry III objected on the grounds that de Melsanby was bound by homage to Robert the Bruce. The matter was even referred to Rome before the monks gave way and selected Nicholas de Farnham.

It was in the mid 1880s when Frith first appear to have sent a cameraman into County Durham, though very few pictures seem to have survived in the archive. There were in-depth visits in 1890 and again in 1892, with Barnard Castle, Durham, Auckland Castle, and Darlington as the main areas, though the Frith photographer also went to Finchale Priory, High Force, Lambton Castle and Lumley Castle. Many of the pictures taken during these visits were intended for publication in the Frith postcard range; hence there are numerous views of Durham Cathedral, of various locations around Barnard Castle, of the waterfall at High

Force, and so on.

It was a time when the North East was an industrial powerhouse: there were coal, iron and steel, shipyards at the forefront of world shipbuilding, and ship repairs. Many towns were economically dependent upon one major employer, just as numerous pit villages were. On the Tyne at Jarrow was the famous yard of Palmer Bros, founded in 1851 by the brothers Charles and George Palmer to build colliers to ship coal to London. In 1852 the yard turned out the world's first sea-going screw collier for the mine-owner John Bowes of Barnard Castle. Carrying 650 tonnes of coal per trip, she could do the work of eight sailing colliers. The firm expanded rapidly, acquiring 14 of its own collieries as well as its own ironstone company and interests in firms that supplied ships' fittings. From 1860 until 1912, Palmers also operated a yard at Howdon, where a considerable number of ships were built. After George Palmer retired, Charles continued to develop the business, opening an engine works, blast furnaces and iron and steel works. The company, which had gone public in 1865, was always innovative. In 1906 electric overhead cranes were installed, and in 1911 the seven-berth Hebburn yard of Robert Stephenson & Sons was leased and eventually purchased. Other acquisitions included a small yard at Amble and the building of a dry dock at Swansea for Palmers

(Swansea) Dry Dock Co.

In 1930, output from British yards totalled 1.4 million tonnes. By 1933, as the Depression hit, it had slumped to 133,000 tonnes. Palmers completed their last merchant ship order in April 1931 and their last warship in 1933. With no prospect of orders, the company went into liquidation. It was a complete closure, including the shipyard, blast furnaces, rolling mills and engine works. Palmers passed into the hands of the National Shipbuilders' Security, a controversial organisation set up by the industry to administer self-inflicted surgery to reduce shipbuilding capacity. Yards were bought and then demolished. The owners were compensated, but their former employees got nothing.

The effect upon Jarrow was disastrous: Palmers was Jarrow. The town was left with nothing. It had the highest rate of unemployment in the entire country, and the government, as usual, offered no help. Men wandered around looking for work that did not exist, while the women as wives and mothers had little time to stand on street corners feeling sorry for themselves; they were forced to scrimp and scrape, to beg or borrow, in the attempt to feed and clothe their children.

There were to be many hunger marches during the 1930s, yet despite being one of the smallest, limited to just 200 men, the Jarrow Crusade has come down to us as being synonymous with the plight of the North-East during the Depression. Organised by the town council and local MP Ellen Wilkinson, the Crusade was an attempt to get the government to take notice of the dire straits Jarrow had been left in with the closure of Palmers. It was left to one man to come to the town's aid. In 1933 Sir John Jarvis, High Sheriff of Surrey, was so moved that he bought a ship due for scrapping and sent it to Palmers. The following year Sir John paid £100,000 for the White Star liner 'Olympic' and then offered her to a Yorkshire scrap metal company for the same amount, providing they agreed to the demolition being done at Palmers. 'Olympic' arrived on the Tyne in October 1935 and provided men with work for eighteen months. Sir John repeated his generous act in 1938 when he bought the Cunard liner 'Berengaria' and sent her to Jarrow for breaking up.

As Jarrow had been dependent upon Palmers, so Consett relied upon its iron and steelworks, and Shildon upon the railway wagon shops. The Consett Iron Co had been founded in 1864 in the aftermath of the collapse of the Northumberland & Durham District Bank, which had seriously undermined established firms such as the Derwent Iron Co. Expansion followed, both in the acquisition of existing plate and tin mills and in the purchasing of controlling interests in coal mines to ensure supplies of coking coal. In 1872,

Consett joined forces with Krupps of Essen, Dowlais Iron Works, and Ybarra of Spain to form the Orcornera Iron Ore Co; this move was designed to guarantee all the partners a supply of ore from the Bilbao area. By 1881, Consett was employing 6000 workers; it also owned ten pits with a combined output of 1.25 million tonnes, producing about half a million tonnes of coke. When Consett closed in 1980, over 4000 jobs were gone, and a town lost its identity. A similar thing happened at Shildon when BR closed the wagon works shortly after its 175th anniversary.

Some areas of the county do not appear to have been visited by Frith until the early to mid 1950s. Pictures of the Weardale hamlets of Daddry Shield, St John's Chapel and Ireshopeburn all date from c1955. When lead was discovered in Weardale, the crown granted mining and revenue rights to the bishops of Durham. By the 13th century, mining, smelting and charcoal burning were on a large scale, and over the next hundred years or so places like Daddry Shield and Ireshopeburn were founded to support an ever-growing population. In the mid 17th century, Upper Weardale became a refuge for Presbyterians, as it was considered remote enough not to arouse any backlash from the authorities. A meeting house and school were built at Ireshopeburn in 1687, and the minister also served a small chapel at Garrigill. During the

1740s and 1750s, Weardale was visited by Christopher Hooper and John Wesley, who between them were responsible for establishing Methodism in the dale. The first Methodist chapel was built in Ireshopeburn, and within a few decades Methodism had become the principal religion of the area.

The pictures of Sunderland were taken between 1890 and 1910. There were a number of yards on the Wear, including William Doxford & Sons, Joseph Thompson & Sons, Short Brothers, and Sir John Priestman & Co. Sir John Priestman, born at Bishop Auckland in 1855, began his career at the age of fourteen when he was taken on as an apprentice at the shipyard of John Blumer & Co. After a period as Chief Draughtsman at Pickersgills, John opened his own yard at Southwick in 1882 and had completed five ships by the middle of 1883. In 1897, the yard completed the first of their 'tower-deck' self-trimming tramps, similar in style to Doxford's 'Turret' ships; these were designed to save shipowners' money on Suez Canal dues, which were charged by deck area. John Priestman became one of Sunderland's great benefactors. He paid for the construction of St Andrew's Church, Roker, and the rebuilding of St Michael's, Bishopwearmouth. During his life, his donations to charitable causes on Wearside amounted to over £500,000, and on his death further money

was left in trust for charitable work.

650 years of shipbuilding on the Wear came to a sad end in December 1988. The last ship built at Sunderland, a 2000 tonne Superflex ferry, slipped into the water at North East Shipbuilder's Southwick Yard just five days after the Government announced the closure of NESL with the loss of 2400 skilled jobs.

As has been already mentioned, Durham is also an agricultural county. In 1968, over 350,000 acres were given over to crops and grasses, of which the largest were barley at 90,000 acres, wheat at 16,000 acres and oats at 12,500 acres. A further 64,000 acres were given over to rough grazing. Livestock returns for the same year show that there were 29,500 dairy cows, 12,500 beef cattle, 332,000 sheep, 59,000 pigs and over 1,355,000 poultry.

This book is not an academic history of the county. The introduction simply sets the scene, while the pictures and their associated captions will, we hope, take you on an enjoyable tour of one of England's most fascinating areas.

Around Darlington

DARLINGTON, ST CUTHBERT'S CHURCH 1892 30641

The first church in the Palatinate in the Early English Gothic style, St Cuthbert's dates from about 1180, when its construction as a collegiate establishment was begun by Bishop Hugh le Puiset. The church is cruciform in plan; the aisles were added during the early 13th century. About a hundred years later the low crossing tower was heightened to house a belfry, and the spire was added.

DARLINGTON

Market Place c1955 D2014

The Great Market Place, as it was once called, is thought to have been laid out by Bishop Hugh le Puiset in about 1164. Though he was the nephew of King Stephen, Hugh was a Prince-Bishop in the true sense of the word. He entered into secret negotiations with William the Lion of Scotland, granting the Scots army free passage across Durham, and allowed French and Flemish troops to land at Hartlepool. Though the rebellion of 1173 failed, Hugh received only a heavy fine and suffered the temporary indignity of having several castles confiscated by the English crown.

DARLINGTON, TUBWELL ROW 1903 50008

Tubwell Row bounds the Market Place along with High Row, St Cuthbert's Churchyard and Horsemarket. On the left are the flower-bedecked premises of the seed merchants and nurserymen Kent & Brydon. Those feeling inspired to practice the green-fingered arts had only to nip next door to Allison the ironmongers, where there was always a ready supply of gardening tools.

DARLINGTON, HIGH ROW 1903 50005

This view of High Row looks towards Bondgate. Over on the left is a branch of the Home & Colonial Stores, which, like Freeman, Hardy & Willis, was one of the early high street chains. Further along on the same side is Taylor's Drug Stores, who had a number of branches north of the Humber.

DARLINGTON, HIGH ROW 1893 32318

We are looking towards the junction of High Row, Houndgate, Blackwellgate and Skinnergate. The street is dominated by the Italianate clock tower, paid for by Joseph Pease; along with the Town Hall and covered market, it was designed by Alfred Waterhouse and built in 1864. In this picture we also see the slope where the fat cattle market used to be held.

DARLINGTON, NORTHGATE 1926 79026

The statue of Joseph Pease stands guard over the entrance to Northgate. Joseph (1799-1872) was the second son of Edward Pease (1767-1858), and was the first treasurer of the Stockton & Darlington Railway. He was also a major influence in the founding and development of the town of Middlesbrough, and was the first Quaker ever to be elected to serve in Parliament.

DARLINGTON, BONDGATE 1906 54444

Bondgate gets its name from the area of the town where the bishop of Durham's bond tenants once lived; it was once a separate manor from Darlington. This picture was taken only a couple of years after the introduction of electric street trams. The tramway had a relatively short life-span - it was closed in 1926.

DARLINGTON, THE TECHNICAL COLLEGE 1898 41661

The Technical College was yet another of G G Hoskins' buildings in the town. Hoskins was also responsible for designing the Grammar School of Queen Elizabeth (1875), John Pease's villa Elm Ridge (1867), the New Hippodrome and Palace of Varieties (1907), and the King's Head.

DARLINGTON
VICTORIA ROAD 1903 50007
This photograph shows Victoria Road and the approach to Bank Top railway station. Designed by William Bell for the North Eastern Railway, this station opened in July 1887, replacing one a short distance to the east.

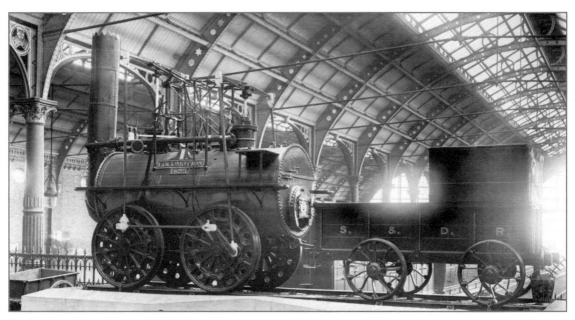

DARLINGTON, S&D RAILWAY NO 1 1892 30646

Designed and built by George Stephenson, Stockton & Darlington No 1, 'Locomotion', achieved a maximum speed of 15mph when she hauled the 34-wagon inaugural train from Shildon to Stockton on 27 September 1825. 'Locomotion' was one of the stars of the S&DR centenary celebrations in 1925, though the old girl was not quite herself; her power came from a hidden petrol engine, and the smoke from her chimney was burning oily waste.

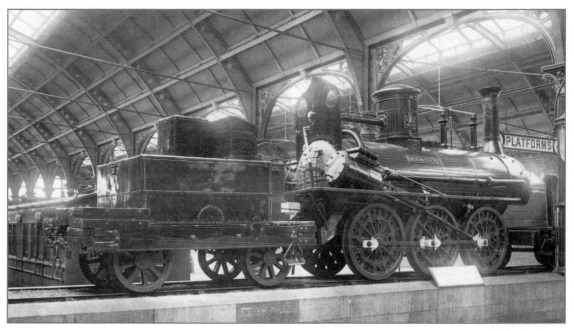

DARLINGTON, THE 'DERWENT' 1901 48014

Designed and built by Alfred Kitchen at his foundry near North Road Station, the 'Derwent' entered service with the S&DR in 1843, two years after 'Locomotion' had been retired. Both locomotives are now housed in the Darlington Railway Centre & Museum, North Road Station.

DARLINGTON
South Park 1896

Opened in 1853, Bellasis Park, as it was then called, was one of the earliest public parks in the north-east. It was named after James Bellasis, a forward thinking man, who as early as 1636 gave Poor Howdens Farm to the town. Between 1880 and 1930 adjoining land was incorporated into the park to give it its present area of about 100 acres.

◆

DARLINGTON
South Park 1911

South Park was renowned for its trees, a number of which were planted to mark special occasions: the sequoias, for instance, were planted in 1863 to commemorate the wedding of Prince Edward and Princess Alexandra. In this picture we can see some of the floral decorations planted to celebrate the coronation of King George V and Queen Mary.

DARLINGTON, SOUTH PARK 1896 37531

DARLINGTON, SOUTH PARK 1911 63549

DARLINGTON, NORTH LODGE PARK 1903 50009

DARLINGTON
North Lodge Park 1903
Entered from Gladstone Street, North Lodge Park is the remnant of the parkland that once surrounded William Backhouse's villa. It opened as a public park in 1901; our picture was taken shortly after the bandstand had been completed.

◆

DARLINGTON
North Lodge Park 1903
Featured here is the fish pond and castellated boathouse that once belonged to William Backhouse; they were retained when North Lodge Park was developed. Keeping the pond topped up was never a problem - it was fed with surplus water from the swimming baths in Gladstone Street. The pond was filled in in 1932, and the boathouse was demolished in the early 1950s.

DARLINGTON, NORTH LODGE PARK 1903 50010

DARLINGTON, THE GRAMMAR SCHOOL 1892 30643

In the early 1870s, the Duke of Cleveland's estate near to the town centre was given over to development. Some of it was used to create Stanhope Park, and it was here that the Grammar School of Queen Elizabeth was built in 1875. The school took in boarders, and its design featured an undercroft playground at one end.

DARLINGTON, WOODLAND ROAD 1892 30640

Woodland Road is better known today as the A68. In the second half of the 19th century, Darlington was growing fast, attracting industry and business. Along Woodland Road were built villas and town houses for the town's business and professional classes.

MIDDLETON ONE ROW c1955 M134003
Before the arrival of the railway, Middleton One Row was aptly named; it consisted of just one row of Georgian cottages. An inn was created by knocking a couple of cottages together, and this later became the basis for the Devonport Hotel, which came into being during the early years of the 20th century.

PIERCEBRIDGE c1955 P150011
Situated six miles west of Darlington, Piercebridge is unusual in that the village was built within the ramparts of a Roman fort that once guarded the bridge over the Tees carrying the road between York and Hadrian's Wall. On the right is the village police house; its high pointed wooden porch looks more like Welsh architecture than that of the north-east of England.

To Bishop Auckland

GAINFORD
The Corner Shop c1955 G102305
Gainford is noted for its 13th-century church, Georgian
houses, narrow streets and one of the finest village greens in
the southern part of the county. Customers at the corner
shop in c1955 would have paid 4d for a 14oz loaf, 1s 3d for a
3lb bag of flour, and 2s 6d for 1lb of butter.

ROKEBY HALL 1903 50037
Completed in 1731, Rokeby was designed by its owner, the amateur architect Sir Thomas Robinson, son-in-law of Lord Carlisle of Castle Howard. Sir Thomas's other work included the Gothic Revival gateway at Auckland Castle and the Mausoleum at Castle Howard.

BARNARD CASTLE 1892 30668
There was a time when Barnard Castle was one of a number of prosperous towns in the Palatinate; the others were Durham, Darlington, Hartlepool, Stockton, Sedgefield, Staindrop and Wolsingham. In the 18th century, Barnard Castle was an important market town and woollen textile centre. Stone-built weavers' houses, carpet weaving mills, and rope works all jostled for space along the banks of the river.

BARNARD CASTLE, MAIN MILL 1914 67182
Barnard Castle had a fulling mill by 1316, which suggests that there was a local cloth industry, and there were three corn mills operating in the 1390s. In the late 1820s the town had a diverse industrial base: there was nail making, tanning, rope making, a dyeworks, five carpet factories, a paper mill, thread mills, and two worsted mills.

BARNARD CASTLE 1890 23075
The Gothic-arched County Bridge straddles what was the old border between Yorkshire and the Palatinate of Durham. Though it is now widely accepted that the bridge was built in 1569, there is a theory that the structure is in fact older, and that the date of 1569 refers to its restoration following damage received during the Rising of the North. The bridge was repaired and given new parapets following severe damage caused by flood waters in 1771.

BARNARD CASTLE 1892 30671

The castle dominates the town. In November 1569, during the
Rising in the North, it was held by Sir George Bowes, a loyal
servant of Queen Elizabeth I, against a force led by Charles Neville,
Sixth Earl of Westmoreland, and Thomas Percy, Earl of
Northumberland. As the rising had popular support throughout
Durham, Sir George's garrison was suspect. Prior to surrendering,
Sir George wrote that his command had been reduced to 'a very
hard dyett and great want of bread, drynck and water; which was
our only drynck, save I myxed yt with some wyne. I fownde the
people in the castle in continuall mutenyes, seaking to leape the
walls and run to the rebells'.

BARNARD CASTLE, BALIOL TOWER 1890 23081
The Round Tower, or donjon, is also known as Baliol Tower. Almost 50ft high and 36ft in diameter, the tower is made of dressed ashlar sandstone and probably dates from the mid 13th century, when polygonal and round keeps were being built in preference to the more traditional rectangular ones.

BARNARD CASTLE, MARKET PLACE 1892 30676
We are looking towards the Butter Market and Barnard Castle's octagonal two-tiered Market Cross, which dates from 1747. It features an open cupola, Tuscan colonnades and a penthouse roof; the ground floor has open archways all the way round.

BARNARD CASTLE, THE BANK 1892 30677
The four-storey gabled house on the right with the flight of steps is Blagroves House. This is now the oldest surviving house in the town. There is a local tradition that Oliver Cromwell briefly used it as his headquarters during late July and early August 1648 when his forces and those of Major-General John Lambert were operating in the area against the Royalists led by the Duke of Hamilton.

BARNARD CASTLE 1914 67169
Trinity Methodist church stands at the bottom end of Galgate, and was completed in 1894. Methodism came to the town during the 1740s and 1750s through the efforts of John Cheesborough and John Wesley. A meeting house was eventually established, and the first chapel was opened by Wesley himself in 1765.

BOWES, DOTHEBOYS HALL 1951 B328003
Dotheboys Hall was where William Shaw ran his notorious Bowes Academy, upon which Charles Dickens based Dotheboys Hall in his novel 'Nicholas Nickleby'. In the churchyard lies George Ashton Taylor, a former pupil of the Academy, who died aged nineteen. Dickens used the unfortunate Master Taylor as the basis for the character of Smike.

RABY CASTLE 1893 32331
Raby is first recorded in the 11th century, and is reputed to have been a royal residence of King Cnut. The castle dates from the 14th century, and was once the seat of the powerful Neville family. It was here in 1569 that the Rising in the North was planned; the intention was to depose Elizabeth I and replace her on the throne with Mary, Queen of Scots.

RABY CASTLE 1893 32329

The plot to overthrow Elizabeth I failed, and Raby became forfeit to the Crown. In 1645 it was bought by the Vane family, who were Royalists. Following a surprise attack, Raby fell to the Parliamentarians, but not to be outdone Sir George Vane retook it, and managed to hold onto it despite being besieged in 1648.

RABY CASTLE C1955 S292006

Built round an internal courtyard, Raby's defences included inner and outer curtain walls surrounded by a broad ditch. It was extensively remodelled during the 19th century by the architect William Burn; it had previously been modernised between 1768 and 1788 by John Carr of York.

STAINDROP, THE VILLAGE c1955 S292001

A collegiate church was founded here by the Neville family of nearby Raby Castle in 1410. Until the late 18th century, the village of Raby and the hamlet of Keverstone lay close to the castle, but they were demolished during improvements that created 270 acres of parkland. The former residents were shipped off to New Raby.

ROMALDKIRK, THE VILLAGE 1898 41447

Situated six miles north-west of Barnard Castle, Romaldkirk in 1898 was not in fact in County Durham but in the North Riding of Yorkshire. The village takes its name from St Romald, the son of a Northumbrian king; he was born in Buckingham in about 800, his mother having taken refuge there during a war between Northumbria and Mercia. Apparently, though Romald lived for only a few days, he was said to already have the power of speech and was possessed of profound and miraculous wisdom.

ROMALDKIRK, THE CHURCH 1898 41449
The parish church features a 12th-century nave and north aisle, and a 15th-century tower. The area around the chancel arch includes some stonework from the village's Saxon church. In 1898 the rector of Romaldkirk also held the title of Lord of the Manor.

EGGLESTON, THE THREE TUNS c1955 E74002
Within the lead-mining area there were smelting mills at a number of locations, including Blagill, Nenthead, Allenhead, Jeffries, Tynehead, and Bollihope. A number of smelters were established outside the area, including Egglestone, Dufton and Hilton.

COTHERSTONE, THE VILLAGE 1898 41445
Cotherstone lies between Lartington and Romaldkirk, and was once a grange belonging to Egglestone Abbey. The Abbey was founded by the Premonstratensians; they were an order noted for preferring secluded areas, both for building their religious houses and for rearing their sheep.

AYCLIFFE, THE GREEN c1955 A112008

In 1940, Aycliffe was one of the locations chosen for the building of a Royal Ordnance Factory. The resulting industrial estate formed the nucleus in 1947 for the creation of Newton Aycliffe New Town. The original development was for a town of 10,000 people, but this was later increased to 25,000.

NEWTON AYCLIFFE, NEVILLE PARADE c1955 N70028

When our cameraman visited Newton Aycliffe, it was still very much a new town and was still being developed by the Grenfell Baines Group. Newton Aycliffe was projected to have five residential districts surrounding a civic and shopping centre, and industry had been attracted to the area - Bakelite had opened a factory as early as 1946.

SHILDON, CHURCH STREET C1965 S704006

Though the North East is readily identified with coal mining, shipbuilding and iron and steel, among its lesser-known industries was the construction of railway locomotives and rolling stock. The principal centres were the North Road Works of Darlington, Shildon Wagon Works, and locomotive manufacturers Robert Stephenson & Hawthorn, who were based at Gateshead. The Wagon Works was Shildon's main employer.

SHILDON, CHURCH STREET C1965 S704005

In 1921, locomotive and rolling stock manufacturing in the North East provided 6300 jobs; by 1951, the figure had risen to 11,000. Then in 1965 BR suddenly closed North Road Works, Darlington. With private locomotive manufacturing also in decline, only Shildon was left with anything like a substantial workforce. Shildon survived as a wagon builders and repairers long enough to celebrate its 175th anniversary, then it too was closed.

SOUTH CHURCH, ST ANDREW'S CHURCH 1892 30714
One mile south-east of Bishop Auckland stands St Andrew's Church. It holds the distinction of being the largest parish church in County Durham. Dating mainly from the 13th century, it features an impressive square west tower, an aisled nave, transepts and chancel. Its treasures include an effigy of a knight dating from c1340 and fragments of an 8th- or 9th-century Saxon cross.

BISHOP AUCKLAND, NEWGATE STREET 1923 74338
Shoppers on Newgate Street in 1923 were seeing prices slowly returning their pre-war levels. In 1914 a pound of butter at the Meadow Dairy Co would have cost 1s 3d; by 1920 the war had pushed the price up to 2s 11d. Similarly, cheese costing 8d a pound in 1914 had hit 1s 8d by 1920, and a dozen eggs had rocketed from 1s 3d to an outrageous 4s 11d.

BISHOP AUCKLAND, SOUTH ROAD 1914 67139

By the 18th century, Bishop Auckland was an important market town at a crossing point of the Wear. Its growth, however, owed much to the development of coal mining to the east and south-west, and later to the north-west. By 1914 the population stood at about 13,000. Markets were held on Thursdays and Saturdays.

BISHOP AUCKLAND, COCKTON HILL ROAD 1914 67138

As numerous pictures in our archive show, traffic was light enough for our cameraman to stand in the road in order to take this image. In the process he appears to have gained the attention of a small group of admirers.

**BISHOP AUCKLAN
NEWGATE STREET 1914** 67136
Newgate Street is one of the features of
the town -it marks the line of a section
of the old Roman road of Dere Street.
In 1914, on the whole the price of basic
food stuffs had been fairly static for ten
years. Tea remained the same at 1s 6d a
pound; there was no change in the
price of flour at 5d for 3lb. Sugar had
fallen from 6d a pound in 1905 to 1d,
but streaky bacon had risen from 9d a
pound to 1s 3d.

BISHOP AUCKLAND, THE GOLF LINKS 1914 67151

BISHOP AUCKLAND
The Golf Links 1914

The years between 1904 and 1914 were boom years for the game of golf - a large number of both private clubs and municipal greens were opened at this time. By the early 1920s Bishop Auckland was one of only a handful of 18-hole courses in County Durham; many, such as Barnard Castle, Felling, Ravensworth, Fence Houses (Lambton Collieries), and Durham City were nine-hole courses. Along with Stockton, it welcomed players from the Ladies Golf Union.

AUCKLAND CASTLE 1892

Once one of the principal fortresses of the Bishops of Durham, Auckland's transformation into a palatial residence began in 1661 when Bishop John Cosin had the 12th-century Great Hall remodelled: he added a clerestory, refaced the exterior and fitted a new roof.

AUCKLAND CASTLE 1892 30706

Auckland Castle 1892 30708

Auckland Castle 1892
Bishop Richard Trevor spent over £16,000 remodelling Auckland. He commissioned the building of the south range, which was completed during the reign of his successor Bishop Egerton.

◆

Auckland Castle Gateway 1898
The gateway was designed for Bishop Richard Trevor by Sir Thomas Robinson, and was completed in 1760. It was the second Gothic Revival building to be completed in County Durham; the style had become fashionable thanks to Horace Walpole, who had used it to great effect at his own house, Strawberry Hill, and the amateur architect Sanderson Miller had used it at Lacock Abbey, Wiltshire.

Auckland Castle Gateway 1898 41459

BISHOP AUCKLAND, NEWTON VIADUCT 1898 41455

BISHOP AUCKLAND, DURHAM ROAD 1929 82521

BISHOP AUCKLAND
Newton Viaduct 1898

Here we see the impressive masonry-arched Newton Viaduct. The county boasted three of the highest bridges on the British railway network (rails above ground or high water level): Deepdale at 161 ft, Hownes Gill at 150 ft, and the Hawthorn at 110.5 ft.

◆

BISHOP AUCKLAND
Durham Road 1929

At this time there is hardly any traffic congestion. By 1925 there were just over a million vehicles of all types on the roads, of which 695,000 were privately-owned cars. Within two years of this picture being taken, private car ownership had risen to over 1,100,000 vehicles. In 1931 there were over 5000 fatal and nearly 130,000 non-fatal accidents.

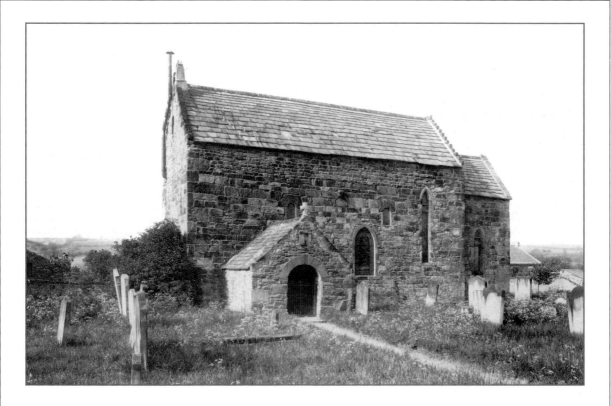

ESCOMB

The Saxon Church 1898 41463

The small 7th-century church of St John the Evangelist is one of
the finest examples of early Christian architecture in the North.
Built largely from stone salvaged from the abandoned Roman fort
at Binchester, St John's lay semi-derelict in the 1870s; it might well
have been allowed to fall into complete ruin, had it not been for
the Reverend R E Hooppell. It was he who recognised St John's
importance and launched an appeal to save it. The long nave and
narrow chancel are typical of Northumbrian ecclesiastical
architecture. Later additions include a 12th-century porch and
13th- and 19th-century windows.

To Durham City

HAMSTERLEY
The Memorial and the Green c1955 H180016
There are two Hamsterleys in the county. One is on the Derwent;
the other is on the Wear. One is a former colliery village and the
seat of the Surtees family; the other appears to be known for the
number of Nonconformist chapels it contains.

WILLINGTON, ST STEPHEN'S CHURCH c1955 W247002
Though the west tower is thought to be medieval, the main body of the church was rebuilt by J A Cory in the 1850s and enlarged between 1869 and 1873.

WILLINGTON, HIGH STREET 1962 W247024
The swinging sixties are still a little way off, but times are changing. Only one of the boys is wearing shorts; the other three are in jeans, which were becoming readily available at around 7s 6d a pair. The roads are free of traffic, but again 1962 would usher in changes. In November the chancellor slashed purchase tax on new cars from 45 per cent down to 25 per cent. The following year car sales topped the million mark for the first time at 1,030,694 vehicles.

WOLSINGHAM, MARKET PLACE c1955 W210016

This view shows the Market Place, with the A689 to Crook on the right and the B6297 to Tow Law on the left. Wolsingham has had a long association with the Roman Catholic faith. There was a time when Catholic priests took their lives in their hands as they travelled Weardale to minister to the faithful. In 1644, Father John Duckett was unfortunate enough to be arrested while on the road between Wolsingham and Tow Law. Duckett was tried and executed.

WOLSINGHAM, THE PARISH CHURCH c1955 W210039

Dedicated to St Mary and St Stephen, the parish church was rebuilt in the late 1840s; all that is left of an earlier 12th-century structure is the lower part of the west tower. The Roman Catholic church, which is dedicated to St Thomas of Canterbury, was designed by J A Hansom, who was also the architect for Birmingham Town Hall; he is best remembered for the Hansom cab.

FROSTERLEY, FRONT STREET c1955 F82002

Situated to the west of Wolsingham on the A689, Frosterley used to be called Forest Lea. For centuries it was the source of Frosterley marble, a fossil-rich crystalline limestone noted for the way it polishes up, and much sought after for church ornamentation.

STANHOPE, FRONT STREET 1969 S293106

Styled the 'capital' of Weardale, Stanhope was once an important centre for the lead-mining industry. By the 1960s, lead-mining in the area had long been consigned to history; it was replaced by quarrying and a growing tourist trade.

EASTGATE-IN-WEARDALE, THE WATERFALL c1955 E72006
Eastgate lies to the west of Stanhope on the A689. The hamlets of Eastgate and nearby Westgate were once the east and west gates of an enclosed deer park belonging to the bishops of Durham, and were probably created for tenants who owed the Bishop service.

DADDRY SHIELD, THE VILLAGE c1955 D91019
When lead was discovered in Weardale, the mining rights were granted to the bishops of Durham; by the 13th century, mining, smelting and charcoal burning and so on were on a large scale for the period. Daddry Shield is just one of several hamlets that grew to support an ever-growing population within Weardale.

St John's Chapel, The Village c1955 S295009

St John's Chapel straddles the A689 between Daddry Shield and Ireshopeburn. The village church, which can be seen on the right-hand side of the picture, was completed in the 1730s, and is unusual in that it has a pyramidal roof.

St John's Chapel, Market Place c1955 S295007

Even when this picture was taken, the hustle and bustle of St John's weekly market lingered on only in the memories of the village's more senior citizens; it had ceased in 1888. The quarterly fairs survived somewhat longer - the last was held in 1908.

IRESHOPEBURN, THE VILLAGE C1955 I67004

The village grew from about the 14th century as people migrated into Weardale following the discovery of iron ore and further veins of lead. Early iron working appears to have been centred upon Cowshill and Ireshope, though in time it spread throughout much of the dale.

HIGH FORCE 1892 30696

Situated five miles north-west of Middleton-in-Teesdale, High Force offers stunning scenery and the spectacular sight of the Tees plunging some seventy feet over the cliffs of Great Whin Sill. The Force has been known to freeze over in the depths of winter.

BRANCEPETH CASTLE 1914 67122
The Neville stronghold of Brancepeth Castle was forfeited to the Crown during the reign of Elizabeth I. In 1633 it was sold by the King's Commissioners and passed through a number of hands; it was bought by the banker and financier William Russell in 1796. It was his son, Matthew, who commissioned the Edinburgh-based architect John Patterson to rebuild Brancepeth, and the work began in 1817.

BRANCEPETH 1914 67121

It was from Brancepeth in November 1569 that the rebel earls of Westmorland and Northumberland launched their attack on Barnard Castle, which was being held for Queen Elizabeth by Sir George Bowes. The earls had even entered into negotiations with the Spanish Ambassador in an attempt to secure assistance from Philip II; the rebels garrisoned the port of Hartlepool. The rebellion collapsed after the earls were defeated near Durham on 15 December.

DURHAM, FROM THE RAILWAY STATION 1892 30728

A train belonging to the North Eastern Railway is about to ease out onto the great viaduct, built by Robert Stephenson in 1857, that carries the line 100 ft above the streets of Durham. The North Eastern had two other stations serving Durham. Elvet closed in 1931 to passenger traffic, but remained open for goods until January 1954. Gilesgate closed to passengers in April 1857 but survived for goods traffic until November 1966.

DURHAM, FRAMWELLGATE BRIDGE 1892 30739

Framwellgate was Durham's first bridge over the Wear. It was built by Bishop Flambard in 1128. The peninsula end was defended by a gatehouse, but this fortification was demolished in 1760. The bridge was rebuilt at the beginning of the 15th century and widened in 1856.

DURHAM, ST MARY-LE-BOW 1918 68230

St Mary-le-Bow is thought to occupy the site of the first Saxon church to be built on the peninsula - this is where St Cuthbert's remains were housed when they were first brought to Durham. The medieval church was badly damaged in 1637 during the collapse of part of the North Bailey. It was rebuilt in 1683, and the tower was added in 1703. St Mary-le-Bow was the parish church for the northern part of the peninsula.

DURHAM, PREBEND'S BRIDGE 1892 30756

DURHAM, THE COUNT'S HOUSE 1914 67129

DURHAM
Prebend's Bridge 1892
Built between 1772 and 1778, the three-arched
Prebend's Bridge replaced a mid 16th-century
footbridge that had been washed away during the
floods of 1771. It was designed by George
Nicholson, architect to the Dean and Chapter of
Durham Cathedral.

DURHAM
The Count's House 1914
Though called the Count's House, this building is
in fact a former summer house dating from about
1820. The original Count's House was about 100
yards nearer to Prebend's Bridge and was the home
of Count Boruwlaski, a Polish dwarf who stood just
39 inches high.

DURHAM, THE CATHEDRAL 1892 30742

We are looking towards the domestic buildings of the Benedictine monastery: the cloisters, dormitory, refectory and kitchen. The building we see between the trees is the refectory, later known as the old library, where a number of relics recovered from St Cuthbert's coffin in 1827 are housed.

DURHAM, THE CATHEDRAL 1918 68213

The battlemented single-storey structure immediately in front of the west portal is the Galilee Chapel, which dates from 1175. Bishop Hugh le Puiset had attempted to build a Lady Chapel at the east end of the cathedral, but construction was plagued with problems, including walls cracking. These events were interpreted as a sign that Durham's saintly misogynist St Cuthbert was angry at the thought of women being allowed so close to his shrine.

DURHAM, THE CATHEDRAL 1892 30741
Dedicated to Our Lord and St Mary the Virgin, Durham is considered to be the finest Romanesque church in Europe. In 1892 the dimensions given were impressive: 510 ft long, 80 ft wide, 170 ft across the transepts, a 240 ft high central tower and two west towers each 138 ft high.

DURHAM, THE CASTLE 1892 30759
To the left is the entrance to the 100 ft long Great Hall built during the reign of Bishop Bek. The corner tower houses the Black Staircase, which when completed in 1662 was free-standing, even though it rises through four floors. In later years the staircase had to be supported with columns owing to a substantial increase in downward weight caused by the building of an additional room on the top storey.

DURHAM, THE CASTLE 1892 30761
A university was officially established at Durham in 1657 during the Commonwealth, but it was suppressed following the Restoration. Durham was finally granted its university in 1832. In 1836 Bishop van Mildbert exercised one of his few remaining powers as a Prince-Bishop by turning over the castle to the university. The keep was reconstructed in 1840 to provide student accommodation.

DURHAM, ELVET BRIDGE 1918 68236

Elvet Bridge was built by Bishop Hugh le Puiset in 1160 to give the peninsula direct road access to the south. It was repaired by Bishop Richard Fox between 1494 and 1501. During the floods of 1771 the bridge was badly damaged, and in 1804-05 the opportunity was taken to widen it. However, it still incorporates some original 12th-century stonework.

DURHAM, OLD ELVET 1914 67127
On the right is that well-known hotel, the Royal County, created in the 19th century out of former town houses belonging to the Ratcliffe and Bowes families. The cast-iron balconies were a feature of town houses belonging to wealthy families. That at No 30 is of particular interest; it afforded the occupants the very best of views of the public hangings that used to take place on Court Green.

DURHAM, THE SHIRE HALL 1921 70730
Built of red brick, the Shire Hall was designed by local architects H Barnes and F E Coates, and was completed in 1898. After the authorities moved out in 1963, the Hall went on to enjoy a new lease of life as the administrative headquarters for the university.

DURHAM, THE SCHOOL 1929 82407
This is perhaps the most famous, and most expensive, public school in the North East. Quite early in the 19th century the University of Durham began offering places to those without means. Hatfield College opened in 1846. Its poor students were provided with furnished rooms, and meals that were taken communally; alien concepts to the well-heeled of Oxford and Cambridge.

From Sherburn to Gateshead

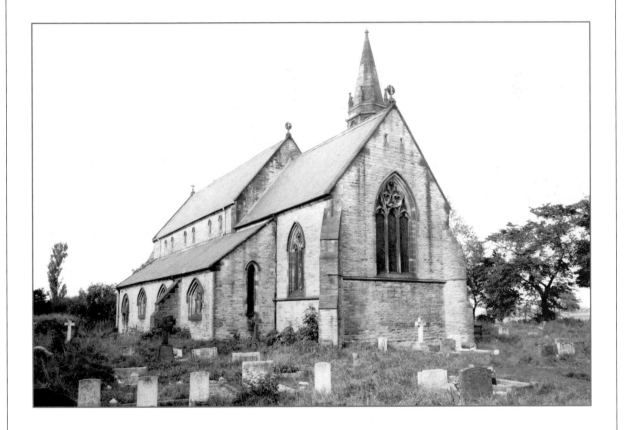

SHERBURN
The Parish Church c1955 S289002

Sherburn was founded in 1181 by Bishop Hugh le Puiset as a
leper hospital, though it later became an almshouse. Little
remains of the original structure save for the south wall of the
chapel. It was redeveloped in the 1760s, and a new master's
house was added in 1832. In the 1860s the architects Austin &
Johnson were commissioned to completely rebuild the church
and main building.

FINCHALE PRIORY 1892 30724

The history of Finchale began in about 1115 when St Godric built himself a hermitage. In about 1150 a chapel dedicated to St John Baptist was added, and on the death of Godric in 1170 at the ripe old age of 105, the site was acquired by the Benedictines of Durham Priory. Before the end of the century Finchale had become a dependent house of about nine or ten monks. A large amount of building work was undertaken during the 13th and 14th centuries, and it appears that Finchale was used as a holiday centre by the monks of Durham. It was dissolved in 1538.

LANGLEY PARK, FRONT STREET c1955 L163021
Langley Park is a pit village just off the road between Lanchester and Durham. The road to the left goes to Quebec and Cornsay Colliery.

LANCHESTER c1955 L160021
The village green, the King's Head and the parish church lie at the heart of present-day Lanchester. Roman Lanchester, or Longovicium, lies half a mile to the south-west; it was one of the principal forts along the road between York and Hadrian's Wall, and was built about the year 122. Though destroyed in 197, it was rebuilt in about 240, and remained in use until the end of the 4th century. Enclosing six acres, the fort was capable of accommodating 1000 troops.

LANCHESTER, THE PARISH CHURCH c1955 L160036

All Saints contains a number of Roman relics, including an altar dating from 244. The chancel was widened and rebuilt when All Saints was granted collegiate status in 1283, and the 15th-century west tower incorporates salvaged Roman stones. The church is noted for its fine sculptures. These include a headless figure of Christ in the tympanum over the vestry door, as well as a number of corbels with carved heads which once served as candle-holders.

CONSETT, MIDDLE STREET c1965 C217003

In 1831 there were only 150 people living in and around Consett. An iron works was opened in 1837, but it was the discovery two years later of ironstone deposits at nearby Shotley Bridge, and the opening of coal pits during the 1840s, that sparked off the town's growth. By 1871 the population stood at around 6000, and by the time this picture was taken it was well over 30,000.

CONSETT, DERWENT RESERVOIR c1965 C217021
Derwent Reservoir lies to the north of Edmundbyers. Not quite a crescent shape, it covers approximately four square miles and is the largest of several reservoirs in the county.

ANNFIELD PLAIN, FRONT STREET 1951 A111001
Annfield Plain, to the north-west of Durham, was one of several towns to attract industrial development as the number of active pits declined. Ransomes & Marles brought jobs to the town when they opened a ball-bearing plant.

CHESTER-LE-STREET, MARKET PLACE c1955 C246001
The tower and spire of the parish church of St Mary and St Cuthbert dominates the skyline in this market day picture. There was a church built of stone on the site as early as 1056; before that, Saxon bishops ruled County Durham from Chester-le-Street's timber-built monastic cathedral, where the bones of St Cuthbert himself were interred from 883 to 995.

CHESTER-LE-STREET, FRONT STREET c1955 C246009
We can see from the size of the bus queues that private car ownership was still something of a novelty. In 1954, sales of new cars in the UK totalled 394,362, with just 4660 imported cars. In 1955 sales were 511,420 with 11,131 imports, but growth was stymied by Government interference. Purchase tax on new cars was increased from 50 to 60 per cent, and purchasers were required to pay a deposit of 15 per cent and the balance over two years.

LAMBTON CASTLE 1892 30715
Lambton Hall is situated to the northeast of Chester-le-Street. Work began in the late 1790s, when William Henry Lambton had an old castle on the site dismantled. The new Hall was designed by Italian-born architect Joseph Bonomi, and was enlarged and completed by his son Ignatius.

LUMLEY CASTLE 1892 30720
Standing just one mile east of Chester-le-Street, Lumley Castle dates from the late 14th century, when Sir Robert Lumley was granted two licences to crenellate. Each of the four square corner towers is topped off with octagonal machicolated turrets. The turreted east gatehouse can be seen through the trees on the right of the picture.

LAMBTON CASTLE 1892 30718
Lambton Hall was castellated and enlarged in about 1833, after which it became known as Lambton Castle. However, in 1854 the paint was hardly dry when it suffered severe structural damage caused by mining subsidence. The rebuilding was undertaken by John Dobson and Sidney Smirke.

HOUGHTON-LE-SPRING, THE BROADWAY c1955 H225006
Hidden behind the trees is the parish church of St Michael and All Saints; burial place of Bernard Gilpin (died 1583), cleric, orator, philanthropist, and founder of Houghton Grammar School. Gilpin came to Houghton after being cleared of charges of heresy, but he was indicted a second time and was on his way to answer the charges when he broke his leg. The accident almost certainly saved him from the stake: while he was recuperating Mary Tudor died, and was succeeded by Elizabeth. The charges were then dropped.

BIRTLEY, DURHAM ROAD C1965 B357031
A number of Co-operative Society factories are located in the North East, the vast majority around Pelaw, where hundreds of products are manufactured, ranging from furniture to clothing and cleaning materials. In 1908 the CWS came to Birtley, where it opened a tinplate works.

WASHINGTON, WASHINGTON OLD HALL C1955 W242013
Washington Old Hall stands next to the parish church. It was here that the ancestors of George Washington were lords of the manor between 1183 and 1376. The hall was greatly altered in the 17th century, and in 1955, following its restoration, it was officially opened by the US ambassador. It is now in the care of the National Trust.

WASHINGTON, THE VILLAGE c1955 W242001

Here we see Washington village about ten years before the area was designated a New Town. There were to be eighteen settlements, or villages as they were to be called, linked together by dual carriageways, for predictions indicated that 'by 1976 it is expected that every family will have at least one car'. By 1981 Washington New Town comprised sixteen villages spread over 5610 acres, and had a population of about 50,000.

WHICKHAM, FRONT STREET c1955 W244004

Whickam is not noted for much save that it was the birthplace in 1748 of William Shield, musician and composer, who rose to become the Master of the King's Music. He was honoured at his death by being buried alongside the great and the good, (and the bad and the mad) in Westminster Abbey.

RYTON, THE TYNESIDE GOLF CLUB c1960 R88010
Often considered to be the prettiest village on Tyneside, Ryton in the early 19th century was a popular residential area for wealthy Newcastle businessmen and merchants, even though it would soon be given over to coal mining.

RYTON, LANE HEAD c1960 R88003
Perhaps the flowerbeds in the foreground are a taste of things to come. In 1968 Ryton won the Britain in Bloom trophy.

WEST BOLDON, ST NICHOLAS TERRACE c1955 W554004
Some of the cottages in St Nicholas Terrace, which is located to the north of the church, are 18th-century, and one of them is dated 1771. The church itself is mid 13th-century and is one of only a handful of churches from this period that retains its broached spire. It seems that when the church was already under construction, the decision was taken to provide it with aisles; evidence of the alteration can still be seen to this day.

WEST BOLDON, GATESHEAD TERRACE c1955 W554001

The area between the south bank of the Tyne and the north bank of the Wear was transformed during the 19th century as coal mines opened and communities grew around them. Nearby Boldon Colliery was sunk between 1866 and 1871, and it was substantially deepened under NCB ownership.

NEWCASTLE, FROM RABBIT BANKS c1898 N16004

This photograph was taken from the Gateshead side of the river. Until 1800, Gateshead comprised little more than three main streets and was the northern end of the County Palatine of Durham. A third of the way along the old bridge over the Tyne were two blue stones; these marked the northern boundary of the Bishop of Durham's jurisdiction.

GATESHEAD, SALTWELL PARK c1955 G124008
Saltwell Park is in the middle of the town, and comprises gardens, a lake, and recreational areas. Saltwell Park Museum is housed in the old mansion. Nearby is the Shipley Art Gallery, named in honour of Joseph Shipley; he not only paid for the gallery, but gave it its private collection of over 500 paintings.

From Jarrow to Stockton

JARROW
Grange Road West c1955 J5001
On the right is the Town Hall, built in 1902 to the designs of the
South Shields-based architect Fred Rennoldson. The area opposite
the Town Hall was redeveloped in the late 1950s by the Arndale
Property Trust in association with Shingler Risdon Associates. They
built a two-storey shopping centre with two wide malls and
covered arcades.

◆

JARROW, THE VIKING STATUE c1965 J5021

This is C M Davidson's sculpture of what are supposed to be a couple of Viking raiders, though they look more like characters from the Games Workshop catalogue. Max Wall would be proud of the legs.
The sculpture forms the centrepiece for the shopping centre.

JARROW, ELLISON STREET c1965 J5029

Jarrow's seven-acre pedestrian shopping precinct opened for business in February 1961; it was all part of a grand scheme to rid the town of its cloth cap image and to drag it into the modern age. The town also embarked upon an ambitious housing programme, replacing older properties with new houses and blocks of flats.

SOUTH SHIELDS, MARKET PLACE c1903 S162009
The old Town Hall, a square building with Tuscan columns completed in 1768, was replaced in 1903 by new municipal buildings designed by E E Fetch. Around the Market Place at this time were a large number of pubs used by the town's seafarers (South Shields had the largest number of seamen as a proportion of its population than anywhere else in Britain) whilst waiting for time to go over to Mill Dam and pay off.

SOUTH SHIELDS, KING STREET c1883 S162010
Unless it was a local custom to stand in the middle of the road, we have no idea what is attracting the attention of the men in the foreground of this picture; surely it is not the horse-drawn tram travelling at a sedate pace along King Street.

SOUTH SHIELDS
KING STREET 1906 S162003
We are twenty years or so on from photograph No S162010. The horse-drawn trams are but a memory, and Isaac Black's famous clothing hall has replaced Greaves & Co, though Liptons and Crofts would be around for some years to come.

SOUTH SHIELDS
KING STREET c1898 S162005
There are bargains to be had at Brash & Willan's, where they appear to be selling off the stock of Wigham & Co (any relation to the shipbuilding firm of Wigham Richardson & Co?). South Shields was not only a port with shipyards and ship repairers; it was also a colliery town, with a pit almost in the town centre.

SOUTH SHIELDS
FREDERICK STREET c1900 S162002
During the first half of the 19th
century, a number of churches were
built to meet the needs of South
Shields' growing population. The
Presbyterian Church, Frederick Street,
was built in 1847. Holy Trinity, Laygate,
was earlier, having been built in 1832-34
to the designs of Anthony Salvin. Both
have since been demolished.

SOUTH SHIELDS, MARSDEN BAY c1955 S162303

WHITBURN, THE GREEN c1955 W245012

SOUTH SHIELDS
Marsden Bay c1955

This was a popular destination for trippers. Marsden has good sands, and is well known for the grotto on the cliff, which also includes a restaurant and a haunted pub. Nearby is Marsden Rock, an arched sandstone rock inhabited by thousands of seabirds.

◆

WHITBURN
The Green c1955

The Green is to the north of St Andrew's Church; around it are some of the village's more interesting houses. The Rectory dates from 1818, whilst Whitburn Hall on the north side, extended and altered in 1856 and 1881, still incorporates parts of a building from c1600.

SEABURN C1960 S340006

Along with Roker, Seaburn comprises what is in effect the seaside resort area of Sunderland, and there have been times when the Cat and Dog steps have positively heaved with sunbathers. A popular attraction during the 1950s were the annual lights along the front and in Roker Park. Those who wanted an inexpensive holiday could book into Seaburn Camp, which even as late as 1960 looked like a film set from a prisoner of war movie, but with flowerbeds.

SUNDERLAND, THE BRIDGES C1900 S263003

A tram rattles across the old road bridge bound for Grangetown. The 236ft single span cast-iron bridge was built between 1793 and 1796, and was considered to be one of the engineering masterpieces of the day. It was replaced by a new Wearmouth Bridge, officially opened by HRH the Duke of York in 1929. Just beyond is the North Eastern Railway's bridge over the Wear.

SUNDERLAND, SHIPYARDS ON THE WEAR c1900 S263508

650 years of shipbuilding on the Wear came to an end with the closure of North East Shipbuilders' Southwick yard in 1989. Here, however, is a reminder of what it used to be like, with ships being fitted out on both sides of the river. Almost hidden in the centre background is one of the tugs belonging to Lambton Collieries and identified by its funnel colours of black with three red horizontal stripes. Around the time the picture was taken, Lambton Collieries were sending between three and four million tonnes of coal a year to the Wear for shipment.

SUNDERLAND, FAWCETT STREET 1890 S263001

This part of Sunderland developed into the commercial and civic heart of the town following the opening of Fawcett Street Station by the North Eastern Railway. In August 1879 both Fawcett Street and Hendon stations were closed on the opening of the new Central Station. In the picture is the Italianate Town Hall designed by Brightwen Binyon; it was demolished in 1971 after being replaced by a new civic centre at West Park.

SUNDERLAND, THE PARK C1900 S263509

This is Mowbray Park, created in the 1850s out of Bildon Hill and the old quarries on its north face. The picture shows the glass and cast-iron winter gardens built on the back of the Library and Museum. This ornate structure was destroyed by enemy bombing during the Second World War.

SEAHAM, THE HARBOUR C1955 S287005

In 1819 Charles Stewart (later the third Marquis of Londonderry) married Frances Anne Vane-Tempest, heiress to an extensive property and coalowning empire. Pretty soon, Stewart was in dispute with the port authorities at Sunderland over handling charges for coal from his Rain collieries. He resolved the matter by buying the small fishing port of Seaham, with the intention of turning it into a coal exporting facility.

SEAHAM, THE HARBOUR c1955 S287008
Colliers await their turn alongside the coal staithes. Nearest the camera is the paddle-tug 'Hardback', which was built in 1901 for the Hodbarrow Mining Co, Whitehaven, and sold to Seaham Harbour in 1925. Her livery was black hull with a yellow line and red boot-topping, buff paddleboxes and superstructure, and black funnel with a yellow band.

SEAHAM, THE HARBOUR c1955 S287007A
We are looking across the old inner harbour to the coal staithes. Partially hidden by one of the staithes is the paddle-tug 'Seaham'. Built for the Seaham Harbour Dock Co in 1909 she spent her entire working life at Seaham before being scrapped in 1962. She was designed so that she could enter the lock and work in the small north basin.

SEAHAM, THE DOCK GATES c1955 S287011

In the 1950s Seaham handled coal traffic from Seaham, Dawdon and Vane Tempest collieries, which between them were producing about 2.5 million tonnes a year and employing around 5000 men. Alongside the staithes is the South Eastern Gas Board's 'Brixton'; awaiting their turn are the 'Thomas Hardie' and the 'Flathouse'.

SEAHAM, CHURCH STREET c1955 S287007

The most interesting church in Seaham is not the one in this picture but St Mary's, which stands on a lonely site on the limestone cliffs. The aisleless nave dates from the late 7th century, and the chancel and west tower from the early 13th century.

SEAHAM c1955 S287004

In 1815 Lord Byron married Anne Isabella Milbanke at Seaham Hall; the marriage is recorded in the church register at St Mary's. Byron hated Seaham; and the marriage was not made in heaven. Of Seaham, Byron wrote: 'Upon this dreary coast we have nothing but county meetings and shipwrecks; and I have this day dined upon fish, which probably dined upon the crews of several colliers lost in the recent gales'.

EASINGTON COLLIERY c1955 E71027

At this time, Easington was one of six large pits situated along the coast of County Durham; the others were Wearmouth, Vane Tempest, Dawdon, Seaham and Horden. Between them they employed over 10,000 men and extracted over 4 million tonnes of coal a year from seams stretching out under the North Sea. Easington closed in 1993.

PETERLEE, YODEN ROAD c1965 P149011

To the south of Easington, the new town of Peterlee was developed with the aim of attracting light industry into the area. The shops here are newly completed, and a number of high street chains such as Dewhurst, Stylo and Woolworths are already in residence. Even the unoccupied units have been let.

CASTLE EDEN DENE 1886 18830

In 1757 Rowland Burdon bought the old manor house and estate of Castle Eden Dene from William Burghley, a former Secretary of State to Queen Anne. Burdon rebuilt the church in 1764 and Castle Eden House in 1786.

BLACKHALL, THE BEACH c1965 B327031

CRIMDON DENE c1965 B327006

BLACKHALL
The Beach c1965

Here we see summer skies and golden sands. However, some areas of the Durham coast were polluted with spoil dumped directly into the sea from nearby collieries. Enterprising locals discovered that wave action separated coal from stone, so there was no need to buy coal when it could be picked for free from the beach; some even turned it into a business. At least one local authority tried to put a stop to the practice, but deservedly fell foul of the common law right to pick sea coals for nothing.

◆

CRIMDON DENE c1965

The wooded valley of Crimdon Dene is an unspoilt area close to Blackhall, where the beach is not polluted with coal spoil. Here in c1965 amenities are basic, though there are toilets and a first-aid hut.

THORNLEY COLLIERY 1951 T123008

When the mining industry was nationalised in 1947, there were 127 active pits in County Durham employing 108,000 mineworkers. Output of the combined Durham and Northumberland coalfield in 1951 was 39 million tonnes, with a productivity level of 259 tonnes per man per year.

COXHOE, THE CROSS ROADS c1955 C249001

Coxhoe straddles the A177 road between Durham and Sedgefield. In the 1950s the village was not dependent upon coal mining for its prosperity, as the quarrying of dolomite (magnesium limestone) was being undertaken in the area on a large scale. Others areas where dolomite was being quarried included Marsden and to the south of Seaham Harbour.

HARTLEPOOL, THE BEACH 1903 49993
A paddle-tug gives a helping hand to two fishing boats. The Tees Conservancy Commissioners were the last tug owners, apart from the Admiralty, to place an order for a paddle-tug. The 'John H Amos' was completed in 1931, having been ordered specifically to work with a recently-acquired floating crane. It was felt that only a paddle-tug could manoeuvre the crane in the confined waters of the Tees. The 'John H Amos' was withdrawn from service in 1967 and presented to the Dorman Museum, Middlesbrough.

HARTLEPOOL, FROM THE PIER 1896 37506

Hartlepool owes its origins to a monastery founded in the mid 7th century. West Hartlepool was a child of the 1830s and 40s, developed as a port for the export of coal and import of timber. By 1851 there were three docks at West Hartlepool, and the Jackson Dock was under construction. At this date the population of West Hartlepool was about 4700; by 1901 it had risen to 63,000.

HARTLEPOOL, SOUTH CRESCENT 1896 37509
Situated to the south east of St Hildas's Church, South Crescent and Albion Terrace were built in the early Victorian period.

FERRYHILL, DARLINGTON ROAD 1959 F81022
Six miles from Durham and twelve miles from Darlington, Ferryhill was only a hamlet until the development of Dean & Chapter Colliery. With the colliery came rows of miners' housing, such as those in Stephenson Street, Bessemer Street, Rennie Street, Davy Street, and Newton Street. By the eve of the Great War there were about 49,000 tied miners' houses in the county housing 260,000 people, or 20 per cent of the county's population.

SEATON CAREW, THE GREEN 1914 67117

The Green was, and still is, one of the more picturesque parts of Seaton Carew; the houses were mostly built in the early 19th century. In the corner, with the steep bargeboarded gables, stands Sylvern House, dating from 1864.

GREATHAM, HIGH STREET c1955 G89004

In the 1950s Greatham consisted of little more than the High Street. In 1272 the Prior of Finchale founded a charity and a hospital here for 'decayed priests'; the local vicar was usually appointed Master. Today the aged and needy do not necessarily have to have been clerics or their widows in order to benefit.

BILLINGHAM, THE SHOPPING CENTRE c1967 B315046

Billingham owes its development to the Great War, when a small chemical works opened nearby for the production of synthetic ammonia for use in explosives. Between the wars the population of Billingham rocketed as the works was expanded for the production of methanol, chemical fertilisers, and petrochemicals. The town centre was redeveloped from the late 1950s by Elder Lester & Partners; the Forum opened in 1967.

STOCKTON-ON-TEES, HIGH STREET c1955 S195002

Stockton was granted its market charter by Bishop Bek in 1310, but until the 1840s it consisted of little more than the High Street, a few side streets, and a quayside railhead for Stockton & Darlington Railway. On the right can be seen the parish church, which dates from 1712. Other 18th-century buildings were the Town House (1735) and the Customs House (1730).

Index

Frith Book Co Titles

www.francisfrith.co.uk

The Frith Book Company publishes over 100 new titles each year. A selection of those currently available are listed below. For latest catalogue please contact Frith Book Co.

Town Books 96 pages, approx 100 photos. County and Themed Books 128 pages, approx 150 photos (unless specified). All titles hardback laminated case and jacket except those indicated pb (paperback)

Amersham, Chesham & Rickmansworth (pb)		
	1-85937-340-2	£9.99
Ancient Monuments & Stone Circles	1-85937-143-4	£17.99
Aylesbury (pb)	1-85937-227-9	£9.99
Bakewell	1-85937-113-2	£12.99
Barnstaple (pb)	1-85937-300-3	£9.99
Bath (pb)	1-85937-419-0	£9.99
Bedford (pb)	1-85937-205-8	£9.99
Berkshire (pb)	1-85937-191-4	£9.99
Berkshire Churches	1-85937-170-1	£17.99
Blackpool (pb)	1-85937-382-8	£9.99
Bognor Regis (pb)	1-85937-431-x	£9.99
Bournemouth	1-85937-067-5	£12.99
Bradford (pb)	1-85937-204-x	£9.99
Brighton & Hove(pb)	1-85937-192-2	£8.99
Bristol (pb)	1-85937-264-3	£9.99
British Life A Century Ago (pb)	1-85937-213-9	£9.99
Buckinghamshire (pb)	1-85937-200-7	£9.99
Camberley (pb)	1-85937-222-8	£9.99
Cambridge (pb)	1-85937-422-0	£9.99
Cambridgeshire (pb)	1-85937-420-4	£9.99
Canals & Waterways (pb)	1-85937-291-0	£9.99
Canterbury Cathedral (pb)	1-85937-179-5	£9.99
Cardiff (pb)	1-85937-093-4	£9.99
Carmarthenshire	1-85937-216-3	£14.99
Chelmsford (pb)	1-85937-310-0	£9.99
Cheltenham (pb)	1-85937-095-0	£9.99
Cheshire (pb)	1-85937-271-6	£9.99
Chester	1-85937-090-x	£12.99
Chesterfield	1-85937-378-x	£9.99
Chichester (pb)	1-85937-228-7	£9.99
Colchester (pb)	1-85937-188-4	£8.99
Cornish Coast	1-85937-163-9	£14.99
Cornwall (pb)	1-85937-229-5	£9.99
Cornwall Living Memories	1-85937-248-1	£14.99
Cotswolds (pb)	1-85937-230-9	£9.99
Cotswolds Living Memories	1-85937-255-4	£14.99
County Durham	1-85937-123-x	£14.99
Croydon Living Memories	1-85937-162-0	£9.99
Cumbria	1-85937-101-9	£14.99
Dartmoor	1-85937-145-0	£14.99
Derby (pb)	1-85937-367-4	£9.99
Derbyshire (pb)	1-85937-196-5	£9.99
Devon (pb)	1-85937-297-x	£9.99
Dorset (pb)	1-85937-269-4	£9.99
Dorset Churches	1-85937-172-8	£17.99
Dorset Coast (pb)	1-85937-299-6	£9.99
Dorset Living Memories	1-85937-210-4	£14.99
Down the Severn	1-85937-118-3	£14.99
Down the Thames (pb)	1-85937-278-3	£9.99
Down the Trent	1-85937-311-9	£14.99
Dublin (pb)	1-85937-231-7	£9.99
East Anglia (pb)	1-85937-265-1	£9.99
East London	1-85937-080-2	£14.99
East Sussex	1-85937-130-2	£14.99
Eastbourne	1-85937-061-6	£12.99
Edinburgh (pb)	1-85937-193-0	£8.99
England in the 1880s	1-85937-331-3	£17.99
English Castles (pb)	1-85937-434-4	£9.99
English Country Houses	1-85937-161-2	£17.99
Essex (pb)	1-85937-270-8	£9.99
Exeter	1-85937-126-4	£12.99
Exmoor	1-85937-132-9	£14.99
Falmouth	1-85937-066-7	£12.99
Folkestone (pb)	1-85937-124-8	£9.99
Glasgow (pb)	1-85937-190-6	£9.99
Gloucestershire	1-85937-102-7	£14.99
Great Yarmouth (pb)	1-85937-426-3	£9.99
Greater Manchester (pb)	1-85937-266-x	£9.99
Guildford (pb)	1-85937-410-7	£9.99
Hampshire (pb)	1-85937-279-1	£9.99
Hampshire Churches (pb)	1-85937-207-4	£9.99
Harrogate	1-85937-423-9	£9.99
Hastings & Bexhill (pb)	1-85937-131-0	£9.99
Heart of Lancashire (pb)	1-85937-197-3	£9.99
Helston (pb)	1-85937-214-7	£9.99
Hereford (pb)	1-85937-175-2	£9.99
Herefordshire	1-85937-174-4	£14.99
Hertfordshire (pb)	1-85937-247-3	£9.99
Horsham (pb)	1-85937-432-8	£9.99
Humberside	1-85937-215-5	£14.99
Hythe, Romney Marsh & Ashford	1-85937-256-2	£9.99

Available from your local bookshop or from the publisher

Frith Book Co Titles (continued)

Ipswich (pb)	1-85937-424-7	£9.99	St Ives (pb)	1-85937415-8	£9.99
Ireland (pb)	1-85937-181-7	£9.99	Scotland (pb)	1-85937-182-5	£9.99
Isle of Man (pb)	1-85937-268-6	£9.99	Scottish Castles (pb)	1-85937-323-2	£9.99
Isles of Scilly	1-85937-136-1	£14.99	Sevenoaks & Tunbridge	1-85937-057-8	£12.99
Isle of Wight (pb)	1-85937-429-8	£9.99	Sheffield, South Yorks (pb)	1-85937-267-8	£9.99
Isle of Wight Living Memories	1-85937-304-6	£14.99	Shrewsbury (pb)	1-85937-325-9	£9.99
Kent (pb)	1-85937-189-2	£9.99	Shropshire (pb)	1-85937-326-7	£9.99
Kent Living Memories	1-85937-125-6	£14.99	Somerset	1-85937-153-1	£14.99
Lake District (pb)	1-85937-275-9	£9.99	South Devon Coast	1-85937-107-8	£14.99
Lancaster, Morecambe & Heysham (pb)	1-85937-233-3	£9.99	South Devon Living Memories	1-85937-168-x	£14.99
Leeds (pb)	1-85937-202-3	£9.99	South Hams	1-85937-220-1	£14.99
Leicester	1-85937-073-x	£12.99	Southampton (pb)	1-85937-427-1	£9.99
Leicestershire (pb)	1-85937-185-x	£9.99	Southport (pb)	1-85937-425-5	£9.99
Lincolnshire (pb)	1-85937-433-6	£9.99	Staffordshire	1-85937-047-0	£12.99
Liverpool & Merseyside (pb)	1-85937-234-1	£9.99	Stratford upon Avon	1-85937-098-5	£12.99
London (pb)	1-85937-183-3	£9.99	Suffolk (pb)	1-85937-221-x	£9.99
Ludlow (pb)	1-85937-176-0	£9.99	Suffolk Coast	1-85937-259-7	£14.99
Luton (pb)	1-85937-235-x	£9.99	Surrey (pb)	1-85937-240-6	£9.99
Maidstone	1-85937-056-x	£14.99	Sussex (pb)	1-85937-184-1	£9.99
Manchester (pb)	1-85937-198-1	£9.99	Swansea (pb)	1-85937-167-1	£9.99
Middlesex	1-85937-158-2	£14.99	Tees Valley & Cleveland	1-85937-211-2	£14.99
New Forest	1-85937-128-0	£14.99	Thanet (pb)	1-85937-116-7	£9.99
Newark (pb)	1-85937-366-6	£9.99	Tiverton (pb)	1-85937-178-7	£9.99
Newport, Wales (pb)	1-85937-258-9	£9.99	Torbay	1-85937-063-2	£12.99
Newquay (pb)	1-85937-421-2	£9.99	Truro	1-85937-147-7	£12.99
Norfolk (pb)	1-85937-195-7	£9.99	Victorian and Edwardian Cornwall	1-85937-252-x	£14.99
Norfolk Living Memories	1-85937-217-1	£14.99	Victorian & Edwardian Devon	1-85937-253-8	£14.99
Northamptonshire	1-85937-150-7	£14.99	Victorian & Edwardian Kent	1-85937-149-3	£14.99
Northumberland Tyne & Wear (pb)	1-85937-281-3	£9.99	Vic & Ed Maritime Album	1-85937-144-2	£17.99
North Devon Coast	1-85937-146-9	£14.99	Victorian and Edwardian Sussex	1-85937-157-4	£14.99
North Devon Living Memories	1-85937-261-9	£14.99	Victorian & Edwardian Yorkshire	1-85937-154-x	£14.99
North London	1-85937-206-6	£14.99	Victorian Seaside	1-85937-159-0	£17.99
North Wales (pb)	1-85937-298-8	£9.99	Villages of Devon (pb)	1-85937-293-7	£9.99
North Yorkshire (pb)	1-85937-236-8	£9.99	Villages of Kent (pb)	1-85937-294-5	£9.99
Norwich (pb)	1-85937-194-9	£8.99	Villages of Sussex (pb)	1-85937-295-3	£9.99
Nottingham (pb)	1-85937-324-0	£9.99	Warwickshire (pb)	1-85937-203-1	£9.99
Nottinghamshire (pb)	1-85937-187-6	£9.99	Welsh Castles (pb)	1-85937-322-4	£9.99
Oxford (pb)	1-85937-411-5	£9.99	West Midlands (pb)	1-85937-289-9	£9.99
Oxfordshire (pb)	1-85937-430-1	£9.99	West Sussex	1-85937-148-5	£14.99
Peak District (pb)	1-85937-280-5	£9.99	West Yorkshire (pb)	1-85937-201-5	£9.99
Penzance	1-85937-069-1	£12.99	Weymouth (pb)	1-85937-209-0	£9.99
Peterborough (pb)	1-85937-219-8	£9.99	Wiltshire (pb)	1-85937-277-5	£9.99
Piers	1-85937-237-6	£17.99	Wiltshire Churches (pb)	1-85937-171-x	£9.99
Plymouth	1-85937-119-1	£12.99	Wiltshire Living Memories	1-85937-245-7	£14.99
Poole & Sandbanks (pb)	1-85937-251-1	£9.99	Winchester (pb)	1-85937-428-x	£9.99
Preston (pb)	1-85937-212-0	£9.99	Windmills & Watermills	1-85937-242-2	£17.99
Reading (pb)	1-85937-238-4	£9.99	Worcester (pb)	1-85937-165-5	£9.99
Romford (pb)	1-85937-319-4	£9.99	Worcestershire	1-85937-152-3	£14.99
Salisbury (pb)	1-85937-239-2	£9.99	York (pb)	1-85937-199-x	£9.99
Scarborough (pb)	1-85937-379-8	£9.99	Yorkshire (pb)	1-85937-186-8	£9.99
St Albans (pb)	1-85937-341-0	£9.99	Yorkshire Living Memories	1-85937-166-3	£14.99

See Frith books on the internet www.francisfrith.co.uk

FRITH PRODUCTS & SERVICES

Francis Frith would doubtless be pleased to know that the pioneering publishing venture he started in 1860 still continues today. A hundred and forty years later, The Francis Frith Collection continues in the same innovative tradition and is now one of the foremost publishers of vintage photographs in the world. Some of the current activities include:

Interior Decoration

Today Frith's photographs can be seen framed and as giant wall murals in thousands of pubs, restaurants, hotels, banks, retail stores and other public buildings throughout the country. In every case they enhance the unique local atmosphere of the places they depict and provide reminders of gentler days in an increasingly busy and frenetic world.

Product Promotions

Frith products are used by many major companies to promote the sales of their own products or to reinforce their own history and heritage. Frith promotions have been used by Hovis bread, Courage beers, Scots Porage Oats, Colman's mustard, Cadbury's foods, Mellow Birds coffee, Dunhill pipe tobacco, Guinness, and Bulmer's Cider.

Genealogy and Family History

As the interest in family history and roots grows world-wide, more and more people are turning to Frith's photographs of Great Britain for images of the towns, villages and streets where their ancestors lived; and, of course, photographs of the churches and chapels where their ancestors were christened, married and buried are an essential part of every genealogy tree and family album.

Frith Products

All Frith photographs are available Framed or just as Mounted Prints and Posters (size 23 x 16 inches). These may be ordered from the address below. From time to time other products - Address Books, Calendars, Table Mats, etc - are available.

The Internet

Already twenty thousand Frith photographs can be viewed and purchased on the internet through the Frith websites and a myriad of partner sites.

For more detailed information on Frith companies and products, look at these sites:

www.francisfrith.co.uk
www.francisfrith.com
(for North American visitors)

See the complete list of Frith Books at:

www.francisfrith.co.uk

This web site is regularly updated with the latest list of publications from the Frith Book Company. If you wish to buy books relating to another part of the country that your local bookshop does not stock, you may purchase on-line.

For further information, trade, or author enquiries please contact us at the address below:
The Francis Frith Collection, Frith's Barn, Teffont, Salisbury, Wiltshire, England SP3 5QP.
Tel: +44 (0)1722 716 376 Fax: +44 (0)1722 716 881   Email: sales@francisfrith.co.uk

---

See Frith books on the internet www.francisfrith.co.uk

TO RECEIVE YOUR **FREE** MOUNTED PRINT

Mounted Print
Overall size 14 x 11 inches

Cut out this Voucher and return it with your remittance for £1.95 to cover postage and handling, to UK addresses. For overseas addresses please include £4.00 post and handling. Choose any photograph included in this book. Your SEPIA print will be A4 in size, and mounted in a cream mount with burgundy rule line, overall size 14 x 11 inches.

Order additional Mounted Prints at HALF PRICE (only £7.49 each*)

If there are further pictures you would like to order, possibly as gifts for friends and family, purchase them at half price (no additional postage and handling required).

Have your Mounted Prints framed*

For an additional £14.95 per print you can have your chosen Mounted Print framed in an elegant polished wood and gilt moulding, overall size 16 x 13 inches (no additional postage and handling required).

---

* IMPORTANT!
These special prices are only available if ordered using the original voucher on this page (no copies permitted) and at the same time as your free Mounted Print, for delivery to the same address

---

Frith Collectors' Guild

From time to time we publish a magazine of news and stories about Frith photographs and further special offers of Frith products. If you would like 12 months FREE membership, please return this form.

Send completed forms to:
The Francis Frith Collection, Frith's Barn, Teffont, Salisbury, Wiltshire SP3 5QP

Voucher for **FREE** and Reduced Price Frith Prints

Picture no.	Page number	Qty	Mounted @ £7.49	Framed + £14.95	Total Cost
		1	**Free of charge***	£	£
			£7.49	£	£
			£7.49	£	£
			£7.49	£	£
			£7.49	£	£
			£7.49	£	£

Please allow 28 days for delivery	*** Post & handling**	**£1.95**
Book Title	**Total Order Cost**	**£**

Please do not photocopy this voucher. Only the original is valid, so please cut it out and return it to us.

I enclose a cheque / postal order for £ . . . .
made payable to 'The Francis Frith Collection'
OR please debit my Mastercard / Visa / Switch / Amex card
(credit cards please on all overseas orders)

Number . . . .

Issue No(Switch only) . . . . .Valid from (Amex/Switch) . . . .

Expires . . . . Signature . . . .

Name Mr/Mrs/Ms . . . .

Address . . . .

. . . .

. . . . Postcode . . . .

Daytime Tel No . . . .   Valid to 31/12/02

The Francis Frith Collectors' Guild

Please enrol me as a member for 12 months free of charge.

Name Mr/Mrs/Ms . . . .

Address . . . .

. . . .

. . . .

. . . . Postcode . . . .

Would you like to find out more about Francis Frith?

We have recently recruited some entertaining speakers who are happy to visit local groups, clubs and societies to give an illustrated talk documenting Frith's travels and photographs. If you are a member of such a group and are interested in hosting a presentation, we would love to hear from you.

Our speakers bring with them a small selection of our local town and county books, together with sample prints. They are happy to take orders. A small proportion of the order value is donated to the group who have hosted the presentation. The talks are therefore an excellent way of fundraising for small groups and societies.

Can you help us with information about any of the Frith photographs in this book?

We are gradually compiling an historical record for each of the photographs in the Frith archive. It is always fascinating to find out the names of the people shown in the pictures, as well as insights into the shops, buildings and other features depicted.

If you recognize anyone in the photographs in this book, or if you have information not already included in the author's caption, do let us know. We would love to hear from you, and will try to publish it in future books or articles.

Our production team

Frith books are produced by a small dedicated team at offices in the converted Grade II listed 18th-century barn at Teffont near Salisbury, illustrated above. Most have worked with the Frith Collection for many years. All have in common one quality: they have a passion for the Frith Collection. The team is constantly expanding, but currently includes:

Jason Buck, John Buck, Douglas Burns, Heather Crisp, Isobel Hall, Rob Hames, Hazel Heaton, Peter Horne, James Kinnear, Tina Leary, Hannah Marsh, Eliza Sackett, Terence Sackett, Sandra Sanger, Shelley Tolcher, Susanna Walker, Clive Wathen and Jenny Wathen.

Free Print – see overleaf